Evil On My Pew:
The Hysteria Around
Sex Offenders In The Church

Larry M. Anderson

Evil On My Pew: The Hysteria Around
Sex Offenders In The Church
Copyright © 2018 Larry M. Anderson
info@larryandersononline.com

All rights reserved. No part of this book may be used or reproduced by any means, graphic, electronic, or mechanical, including photocopying, recording, taping or by any information storage retrieval system, without the written permission of the publisher except in the case of brief quotations embodied in critical articles and reviews.

Entegrity Choice Publishing
PO Box 453
Powder Springs, GA 30127
info@entegritypublishing.com

The views expressed in this work are solely those of the author and do not necessarily reflect the views of the publisher, and the publisher hereby disclaims any responsibility for them.

All of the characters, names, incidents, organizations and dialogue in this novel are either products of the author's imagination or are used fictitiously.

ISBN: 978-0-9991780-4-1

Library of Congress Control Number: 2018932968

Printed in the United States of America

Dedication

This book is dedicated to all the families and individuals who have been abandoned by church leaders and members as result of inclusion on the sex offender registry, and also to those who chose to abandon their faith in God because they felt the pain of sexual sin was too much to bear.

Acknowledgements

I am appreciative to everyone who has inspired, encouraged, and pushed me to complete this book. It's too many to name individually. I appreciate your love, kindness, and generosity. A humble thanks to each and every one of you!

Contents

Dedication 3
Acknowledgements 5
Introduction 11

Part 1
The Issue: Addressing how most churches are adopting a secular view in dealing with registered sex offenders

Chapter 1
Defining The Problem 17
   Legal and Spiritual Repercussions 21

Chapter 2
Biblical Approach 25
   Eyeballing Predator Panic.......................................27
   A Plague? 28
   For Every Five, is One at Risk? 29

Chapter 3
Revisiting Retrogression 31
   Reasons Behind the Hysteria 34
   Moral Fears 35
   Apprehensive Laws 36
   Tragically Misleading 37
   Dealing With F.E.A.R. 39

Part 2
The Impairment: Dealing with the residual effects of the issue regarding the growth of the ministry and the individual

Chapter 4
When Sex Offenders Attend Church 43
   From Indifference to Action 46

Chapter 5
Residual Damage 47
   Sex Offenders in Church: To Ban or Not to Ban? 49

Chapter 6
Where is Grace? 53

Biblical View 54

Part 3
The Resolve: Helping the church come to a place of repentance, love, and acceptance

Chapter 7
How Are Churches Ministering to Society's Most Despised? 61
    Life After Prison 63
    Going Beyond the Risk Involved 63
    Trust and Verification Go Hand in Hand 64
    The Road to Redemption 65
    Case in point 65

Chapter 8
Hostility Towards Sex Offenders: Brief History 67
    Specific Incidences of Violence Against Sex Offenders 68
    There is Hope Even (Especially) For the Sex Offender 69

Chapter 9
The Role of the Church 71
    Watchful Grace: 74
    Are Sexual Sins Bigger Than God's Forgiveness? 78
    Christ's Cross and Sex Offenders 79

Chapter 10
Biblical Guiding Principles In Dealing With Sex Offenders 81
    We Are All Sinners Saved By Grace 82
    Receive Those Whom Christ Receives 83
    More Verses to Show Why We Should Accept Those with Offenses 84
    Some Biblical Reasons for Setting Limitations 84
    Protecting the Congregation 85
    Risk Assessment 85
    Shepherd the Offender 86

Introduction

I grew up in a small city south of Nashville, Tennessee. I'm the youngest of four kids and was raised by parents who always taught me how to love and respect others. I can remember the clarion feelings of acceptance as a child whether, in school with classmates, at church with other congregants, or just at play with friends in my neighborhood. Early one Tuesday morning as I prepared for school my excitement was building because there was news the day before that the Super Friends were coming to town.

Like most kids in my neighborhood we lived for sugary treats, a host of comics, and the treasured Saturday morning dose of Super Friends. What added to my excitement was the fact that the entire Super Friend cast would be landing by plane at the airport within eye distance of my home. Opening the front door, I was startled by a huge figure outside. As I recovered from my initial shock, I realized I was standing face-to-face with the Werewolf character who had a few cameo roles in the Super Friends line up. I stood, looked, and thought in my 8-year-old mind, "This has got to be my imagination".

I quickly turned my head left, and as I moved, he moved. I moved my body and the werewolf mimicked my every move. That's when the fear set in. Up to this point in life, I hadn't been shaken by many things. I closed the door and ran to tell my sister that the Super Friends Werewolf was at the door. I told her how when I moved he moved. At the time she was on the phone with my mother who, along with my dad, worked an early first shift job. So, my mother sent my sister to see what I was seeing and to my amazement, she came back to the phone and reported that there was no Werewolf.

By this time. I'm desperately pleading my case with my mom and refusing to go out the front door to catch the school bus. So, my mom convinces me that if I don't get out of that door to catch the bus there will be consequences. Finally, I mustered all my strength and went to the door. When I opened the door, he was still there. I stood, looked, and moved again, and just like before he mimicked my every move and gesture. I frantically closed the door trying to figure out what went wrong and how he ended up at my front door. Was he lost? How did he get separated from his friends, and on and on?

I couldn't figure it out, but I knew I had to get out of that door. Once again, I muster my strength and opened the door. I look him face to face, close my eyes, bolt through the door, and run. As I ran down the street, there was a comfort surrounding me and I felt a power lift me and carry me to the bus stop. My classmates and neighborhood friends began to ask why I was running so fast and so hard, but I didn't have the words to explain what I had just experienced. Feeling kind of emotionally stuck in the moment, I asked my best friend if he believed in God, and he replied, "Yes, I believe in God." So, I shared my story with him about coming face to face with Werewolf. I also shared with my friend that I felt like it wasn't me running but that I had been lifted by a power to bring me to the bus because of my fear of Werewolf.

I wish I could say that I had figured out why I saw the Werewolf character at my door that morning, but I can't. What I do know for certain is that my trust in God was being developed at a very early stage of my life. Years passed before I was faced with another unexplainable event. In the summer of 2007, I received a phone call from a friend who worked for the local sheriff's department. She stated that she had just heard my name in a conversation from a sexual assault detective and that they were planning to come to my house because there was a girl claiming to have been raped by me. My initial response was just like the moment I opened the door and stood face to face with Werewolf.

I stood, and I looked, but this time I was frozen. I couldn't move or speak. Shortly thereafter detectives arrived at my home. They asked question after question, probing to see if there were any inconsistencies in my story. They gathered sheets from my bed, a few pieces of clothing from my room, and left. Ten months passed, and I made the decision to release my attorney. He agreed, stating if they had any real evidence I would already have been arrested. Ironically, the very next morning I was arrested for rape and statutory rape.

Although I made bail the same day, I was completely devastated by this allegation against me. Upon my release, I was summoned by the elders and pastors of my church. They wanted answers.

I understood their position, so I freely and openly shared with them my shock in the matter. They decided to share it publicly and immediately I could sense a change in the air. The leaders, church mothers, elders etc. seemed to slowly withdraw from myself and my family. Shortly thereafter, I met with the elders, again, and was informed that my pastoral gift would no longer be acknowledged in the assembly due to my arrest. Again, I understood their position.

Days turned into months and months into years before the case was resolved. Periodically, the church's finance team would bring me a check to assist with bills and other expenses for my kids. Fast forward 5 years, and I had pretty much accepted that my gift might never be used again. I spent many years trying to figure out why I was standing face to face with this horrible lie. But, on a Tuesday morning while attending a biblical training session my hopes and dreams were restored by encouraging words from a senior pastor whom I didn't know. He lived 700 miles away from the city where I lived. He simply said, "God has a bigger plan for you." As he started to describe the plan and the people I would serve, I embraced this revelation with open arms. I opened the door and ran, and as I ran, I remembered my experience with the Werewolf at my front door all those years ago, and how the power I now know as God lifted and carried me to my destination.

I wrote this book to encourage the many individuals like myself who have been faced with the scrutiny of a sexual offense and the hurt of being shunned by the people who should love you and care for you unconditionally. Although my church experience has been exceptionally positive, there are still many who are suffering and in need of a place to connect and restart their lives. My prayer is that this book will help them find the Right Church at the Right Time.

There are places and systems in our journey that may never develop a sensible, workable strategy for individuals who are ensnared by sexual sin. My hope is that this book is a catalyst – the beginning of helping Pastors, Leaders, and Churches worldwide develop strategies and insights that will empower and restore families and individuals, while pleasing God and advancing His Kingdom. My fervent hope is that there will come a day when we all run to the life-affirming freedom found only in Jesus Christ. I pray this book will spark a much-needed conversation among pastors and church leaders, and that they, in turn, will address the issue from a clear Biblical perspective and not from a secular one. God's Word promises grace, healing, and restoration for all who call upon Him. With His help and guidance, this book will help foster those Kingdom promises.

Part 1

The Issue: Addressing how most churches are adopting a secular view in dealing with registered sex offenders

1
Defining The Problem

In the small town of Franklin, Louisiana, a man was accused of raping a 13-year-old girl who had gone to him looking for money to buy food. The girl had done this with various men in town before. This time, however, when her mother caught her counting the money that she had received, she told her mother where the money came from and her mother reported the incident to police. The police arrested the man but released him a week later on bond.

While he awaited a trial date, the man and his family began attending a local church. The church was warm and welcoming towards the family, even allowing the man and his wife to christen the child of one of the congregation members. In this environment, the man gave his life to Christ and his teenage boys followed suit. The church members stood and clapped, congratulated him on taking this step, and some even embraced him and the boys.

A week later, the man decided he wanted to take another step towards the kingdom. When the pastor opened the doors to the church, he and his family stood and went to the altar. He expected the same warm embrace that he had previously received. The man had been attending services for a month, had contributed to the building fund and the benevolent fund. His boys were actively attending Sunday school and other youth activities. His wife hoped to join the choir or perhaps become an usher, but the congregation has to vote new members in, under the charter of the church.

This was usually a formality. Which means, surely no one would stay seated when the time came. The pastor asked all those in favor of allowing the man and his family to join the congregation to stand. Two people stood, while the others remained in their seats. The pastor, thought perhaps they had not understood, so he asked the question again. The women shifted uncomfortably in their seats and men grabbed their daughters' hands and shook their heads. Apparently, having the alleged sex offender and his family participate in services was one thing, but openly extending membership was another. Embarrassed, the man and his family left the church and did not return the following Sunday.

The church needs to have an emergency meeting about sex abuse that extends not only to the victims, but also to the offenders themselves. Sex abuse is a widespread problem that damages not only the victims but also their families and communities at large. While the automatic responses to the question of how to address the subject range from "imprison, torture and murder" the offender to "pray for him and hope it gets better", neither of those responses comes close to adequately handling this issue.

Because in recent years, the media has shone a spotlight on Catholic priests who have been accused of molesting young parishioners, many think of sex abuse in the church as a Catholic problem. They think that their churches are immune from such scandals, and are shocked when prominent ministers from other denominations are similarly exposed. The truth is that statistically, 1 in 4 women and 1 in 6 men were victims of sexual abuse as children. So, regardless of the denomination, if your church has 200 people, at least 41 of them have been abused.[1] Since most abusers are family members or others that children know, and about 93 percent of sex offenders consider themselves religious, there is a strong chance that they were victimized by someone in their churches. It is also likely that there are children in your church being abused by someone in the church.

That is not even to say that this problem only affects children. In a 1994 study of men and women released from prison, 9,700 of the men were sex offenders with only 4,300 of them having

---

[1] Tchividjian, B. "Startling Statistics: Child abuse and what the church can begin doing about it," Religion News Service, http://boz.religionnews.com/2014/01/09/startling-statistics/

been identified as child molesters. That means that while you might not be sitting next to a child predator, you may still be attending services with a sexual predator of some sort. The thought is enough to send many into a panic.

Despite Jesus' teachings that all are worthy of salvation and redemption, those who are identified as sex offenders are often seen by both the church and by the world at large as irredeemable. It can be difficult to think otherwise, because 5.3 percent of men released from prison after having served time for sex crimes go on to get arrested again for another sex crime.[2] The natural instinct, when faced with the possibility that a sex offender might re-offend, is to be both fearful and repulsed at the thought. Strangely, though, when faced with any other sin or crime, the response from the church is different. Even murderers, we believe, can be saved by grace through Jesus Christ. According to 2 Corinthians 5:17, anyone who is in Christ is a "new creature" and can look forward to a new life.

"Therefore, if anyone is in Christ, the new creation has come: The old has gone, the new is here!" 2 Corinthians 5:17 NIV

Yet, we look with skepticism at the salvation experience of a sex offender as though the scripture said or implied "anyone, that is, except for him."

The Function of This Book

While this book is an attempt to address the problem of sex offenders in the church from a standpoint of redemption instead of condemnation, it is not an apologetic for child molesters. It should not be viewed as offering excuses for those who violate the sacred trust of the vulnerable in their midst, nor as a work that dismisses the pain suffered by those who have

---

[2] Office For Review of Sexual Misconduct Allegations, "Registered Sex Offenders in the Church: A Guide for Parishes", https://oca.org/PDF/sexual-misconduct/2014-04-reg-sex-offender-parish-guide.pdf

been abused. It is also not meant to be a comprehensive manual on church policy towards the issue addressed.

This book should, instead, be employed as a tool to spark a much-needed discussion among church leadership and members concerning how to deal with a problem that is pervasive and destructive among the body of Christ. Things that continue to be covered up as the problem of sex abuse in the Church has become festering wounds with no chance of healing. It is only by opening up a dialogue that we can begin to find solutions to the problem and move forward.

Legal and Spiritual Repercussions

Christ Tabernacle Missionary Baptist Church in Jacksonville, Florida was faced with a difficult decision when Pastor Darrell Gilyard was hired to conduct services at their church. Because he was an admitted child molester who had abused one girl at his previous church and sent lewd messages to another girl. He could not legally preach in a congregation that included children. So, they did what seemed logical to them at the time: they banned children from their services. In 2014, a judge modified the terms of his probation to allow him to minister with children present as long as there were other adults to supervise their interactions.[3]

This case is certainly an extraordinary one. A 2010 study conducted by Christianity Today International revealed that out of 2,864 respondents, eight in ten thoughts that a sex offender should be included as a participant in church services but under supervision and with certain limitations. The limitations placed on sex offenders include rules against being placed in leadership positions, especially in roles that would include authority over children. 37 percent of those who responded include known sex

---

[3] Allen, B. "Probation Terms Altered to Permit Sex Offender Pastor to Minister to Children," Baptist News Global, https://baptistnews.com/ministry/people/item/28621-sex-offender-pastor-can-minister-to-children

offenders in their services but with certain conditions imposed. Only two percent stated that sex offenders are completely excluded from their services.

Legally, the subject of having sex offenders attend services that include children is a touchy one. After all, many are subject to probationary terms that include not living or being in places where children gather. There are also other considerations involved in the way that the church handles this issue. One of them is that of insurance carriers that protect the churches from catastrophic events.[4] Set Free Christian Church in Medford, Oregon went to battle with their insurance company, Church Mutual, because of the company's requirements which included revealing the identities of the sex offenders in the congregation to all members and only allowing these offenders to attend one service per week with an escort. They would also not be allowed to participate in youth programs.[5, 6]

No one disputes the fact that children have to be protected from those who would seek to harm them. The issues have more to do with the law and the application of the law with regards to registering sex offenders. Under the law, both a thirty-year-old male who has sex with a 12-year-old girl and an 18-year-old male who has sex with his 17-year-old girlfriend may be charged and convicted as sex offenders. Though their circumstances are different, neither the law nor the insurance companies make those distinctions.

There must be a balance between protecting victims and treating every offender as though they are seeking someone to

---

[4] Hammar, R. "Setting Boundaries For Sex Offenders to Attend Church," Christianity Today, http://www.churchlawandtax.com/blog/2012/july/setting-boundaries-for-sex-offenders-to-attend-church.html
[5] Althof, A. "Insurance Carrier Orders Church How to Treat Sex Offenders," Christianity Today, http://www.christianitytoday.com/gleanings/2012/july/insurance-carrier-orders-church-how-to-treat-sex-offenders.html
[6] Specht, S. "That's Not Why I'm Here," Mail Tribune, http://www.mailtribune.com/apps/pbcs.dll/article?AID=/20120624/NEWS/206240323

prey upon in the congregation. Not all who have been accused of sexual abuse are automatically guilty, so the church risks ostracizing members who are as innocent as those they are seeking to protect. Another problem with this approach is the fact that offenders who are singled out, isolated and treated as though they will never change have no way of reintegrating into the society that they may have already been isolated from in prison. If they are only allowed in churches with escorts, this is not much different from being walked from one area of a prison to another by a guard. How will they learn proper interactions with all age groups if they are not allowed to have any?

One other danger that neither the insurance company nor the law has addressed properly is that of driving offenders underground. If they see that they will be targeted and persecuted for the crimes that they committed even after being released from both prison and having fulfilled the conditions of their probation (which include registering as sex offenders), many will simply choose not to disclose their identities. While this might be a hard task in a small town where everyone knows everyone, in a larger city with larger churches it is easier to become invisible. This invisibility makes it easy both for former offenders to interact without any kind of supervision and to re-offend because there is no way to seek help without revealing the reason they need it.

2

Biblical Approach

The church is supposed to hold itself to a different standard from the world in all cases. While they may offer some guidance to keep the church out of legal trouble, neither insurance companies nor law enforcement should be allowed to completely dictate church policy. Church policy needs to be guided primarily by the Bible.

In 1 Peter 5:8, we are told to be "alert and of sober mind" because the devil is always looking for someone to destroy.

"Be alert and of sober mind. Your enemy the devil prowls around like a roaring lion looking for someone to devour." 1 Peter 5:8 NIV

There is no way to know if someone who has committed a sex crime will do so again. Therefore, it is necessary to exercise caution and be vigilant when there is a known offender among the congregation. Of course, because not all who have committed sex crimes have gotten caught, it is necessary to be cautious with anyone who works with children and other vulnerable church members. However, turning a lookout into a witch hunt for potential predators is both unnecessary and counterproductive. Instead, churches should adopt policies that keep potential predators from exercising authority over children, provide adequate supervision for all youth activities and create avenues for youth to discuss things that may have been said or done by those in charge to make them feel uncomfortable.

When an offender is repentant, it is also important not to condemn him by actions or words. There is a temptation, in the name of justice, to continually remind a person who has committed a heinous crime of what he did. However, one who has truly repented has experienced "godly sorrow" that has led him to salvation.

"Godly sorrow brings repentance that leads to salvation and leaves no regret, but worldly sorrow brings death." 2 Corinthians 7:10 NIV

He is fully aware of what he did and understands the consequences.[7, 8] It is not up to us to continue to remind him but to help him move forward and live a godly life. Those who are strong are instructed to "bear the infirmities of the weak" and "build them up".

"We who are strong ought to bear with the failings of the weak and not to please ourselves. Each of us should please our neighbors for their good, to build them up." Romans 15:1-2 NIV

That means that we are to provide help and support to both offenders and victims of sexual abuse in the church. It is only then that we can begin to see them healed.

Eyeballing Predator Panic

Real and perceived threats have propelled the society to develop panic over predators. The American people scramble to protect their children from a wide array of dangers counting school gunmen, online bullying, violent computer games, snipers, Satanic Ritualistic Abuse, drugs, pornography, and the Internet.

Taxpayer dollars in the hundreds of millions have been used protecting minors from one threat or other, hardly ever pausing to observe how costly or helpful the remedies are - or the actual severity of the threat in the first place. So, it is with America's most modern fear: sexual predators.

Listen to lawmakers and the daily news reports and you'll be drawn into the panic. According to them, sexual predators lie in wait everywhere: at schools, in parks and the malls - including children's bathrooms, bedrooms and over the Internet. Some

---

7 Liautaud, M. "Sex Offenders in the Pew," Christianity Today, http://www.christianitytoday.com/ct/2010/september/21.49.html
8 Tchividjian, B. "4 lessons we can learn from a church that hired a sex offender," Religion News Service, http://boz.religionnews.com/2014/06/27/4-lessons-learn-church-just-doesnt-get/

rare, but high-status incidents have produced an extraordinary flood of new laws passed in response to the public's fright. Each state has announcement laws to notify communities about known sex offenders. In many states, such individuals have been banned from living in certain areas, and are tracked using satellite technology. Other states have gone several miles further; for example, Florida and Texas state emergency leaders are creating procedures to route convicted sex offenders away from communal emergency shelters during hurricanes. Texas Homeland Security Director Steven McCraw (now retired) said, "We don't want them in the same shelters as others." Although it is unclear just how thousands of desperate and homeless tempest victims are to be identified, filtered, and routed in an emergency.

A Plague?

One of the worst epidemics I can think of at the moment, besides the 10 plagues[9] and the AIDS scourge is the bubonic pandemic[10] which resulted in the deaths of an estimated 25 million (6th-century outbreak) to 50 million people (two centuries of recurrence).[11, 12]

To many people predators are a menace and consider this not only a real but serious pandemic. Senate Majority Leader (2003-2007), Bill Frist said, "the danger to teens is high." And several people believe that this is especially true on the Internet. It is no wonder officials have made launching raids and arrest sweeps a top priority.

---

9   Water to blood, frogs, gnats or lice, flies, livestock disease, boils, hail, locusts, darkness and death of the firstborn (Exodus 7:14-11:1-9)
10   http://www.history.com/topics/black-death
11   Rosen, William (2007), Justinian's Flea: Plague, Empire, and the Birth of Europe. Viking Adult; pg 3;
12   Moorshead Magazines, Limited. "The Plague Of Justinian." History Magazine 11.1 (2009): 9-12. History Reference Center

Jim Acosta, a CBS Evening News broadcast correspondent reported the following on April 18, 2005: "When a child is missing, chances are good it was a convicted sex offender." But the truth is that if a child goes missing, a registered sex offender is among the least likely explanations, far in the rear of runaways, family abductions, and the child being lost or injured. Dateline reporter Chris Hansen, on his NBC series "To Catch a Predator," stated that "The scope of the problem is immense," and "seems to be getting worse." Hansen asserted that Internet predators are "A national epidemic," while the FBI estimates 50,000 predators online[13] at any given moment, all looking for potential victims.

Evidently, sex offenders are a real threat and commit horrendous crimes. Those who prey on children are dangerous, but how widespread and great is the danger? In spite of everything, the world has many dangers - from natural disasters to animal attacks to senseless random shootings - that are genuine but somewhat isolated. Let's look at some widely recurrent claims about the threat posed by known sex offenders.

For Every Five, is One at Risk?

On May 3, 2006, ABC News, citing the prevalence of Internet predators reported, "One in five children is now approached by online predators." However, this is not accurate because the "One in five statistics" can be traced back to "The Youth Internet Safety Survey", a 2001 Department of Justice study issued by the National Center for Missing and Exploited Children that asked 1,501 American minors between 10 and 17 about their online experiences. The casual observer missed this picture.

---

13 We must also remember that "online" is much more than spending time on the computer. Now smartphones and even video games are completely connected to the outside world.

"Almost one in five (19 percent) ... received an unwanted sexual solicitation[14] in the past year." None of the reported solicitations led to any actual sexual contact or assault. Moreover, almost half of the "sexual solicitations" came not from "predators" or adults but from other teens - what can be the equivalent of teen flirting. When the study examined the type of Internet "solicitation" parents are most concerned about (for example, someone who asked to meet the teen somewhere, called the teen on the telephone, or sent gifts), the number dropped from "one in five" to just 3 percent. This is a distant cry from an epidemic of children being "Approached by online predators." As the study noted, "The problem highlighted in this survey is not just adult males on the prowl for sex. Much of the offending behavior comes from other youth [and] from females." Furthermore, "Most young people seem to know what to do to deflect these sexual come-ons." The reality is far less grave than the ubiquitous "one in five" statistic suggests.[15]

---

14   A "sexual solicitation" is defined as a "request to engage in sexual activities or sexual talk or give personal sexual information that was unwanted or, whether wanted or not, made by an adult." Using this definition, one teen asking another teen if he or she is a virgin - or got lucky with a recent date - could be considered "sexual solicitation."

15   https://www.ncjrs.gov/pdffiles1/ojjdp/fs200104.pdf

3

Revisiting Retrogression

When we get saved, we are expected to grow and this growth happens over a period of time. The better support we have the stronger and more stable we get, otherwise we backslide - returning to our former ways. Is this any different with the sex offender? Is it just because they sinned differently than we did that we think we are more acceptable than they are?

A great deal of the concern over known sex offenders arises from the opinion that since they have committed one or more sex crimes before, they are almost sure to engage in others. This is the main reason given for why sex offenders (rather than, say, armed robbers, gangsters or murderers) ought to be monitored, scrutinized and segregated from the public upon their release from prison. The truth is that serial sex offenders, similar to serial killers, are by definition likely to strike again, but what are the facts about sex offenders committing further sex crimes?

It is often repeated that there is a high recidivism[16] rate among sex offenders and we have now accepted it as truth, while in reality, recent studies show that sex offenses rates of relapse into criminal behavior are not unusually high.

"Recidivism of Sex Offenders Released from Prison in 1994", a U.S. Bureau of Justice Statistics study reports that just five percent of sex offenders followed for three years after their release from prison in 1994 were arrested for another sex crime.[17] Another study released in 2003 by the Bureau of Justice Statistics found that within three years, 3.3 percent of the released child molesters were arrested again for committing another sex crime against a child.[18] While not belittling its seriousness, three to five percent is hardly a high repeat offender rate.

---

16 Recidivism is the act of re-engaging in criminal offending despite having been punished.
17 http://www.bjs.gov/content/pub/pdf/rsorp94.pdf, http://www.bjs.gov/content/pub/press/rsorp94pr.cfm
18 http://www.bjs.gov/index.cfm?ty=pbdetail&iid=1136

In the largest and most comprehensive study ever done of prison recidivism, "State of Recidivism: The Revolving Door of America's Prisons"[19], the Justice Department found that sex offenders were, in fact, less likely to re-offend than other criminals. This study comprised of nearly 10,000 men convicted of rape, sexual assault, and child molestation found that sex offenders had a 25 percent lower re-arrest rate than for all other criminals. Partly because serial sex offenders (those who pose the greatest threat) hardly ever get released from jail, and the ones who do are unlikely to re-offend. If released sex offenders are in actuality no more likely to re-offend than armed robbers, gangsters or murderers, it gives the impression that there's little justification for the public's panic and monitoring laws targeting them. Are sex offenders who live near schools or playgrounds more likely to commit additional sex crimes than those living elsewhere?

To answer that, a 2008 study from Lynn University, the University of New Mexico and the University of Nevada researched recidivism rates among Florida sex offenders. It did not find a correlation between the offenders' homes in proximity to schools and playgrounds and their likelihood of re-offending. The study concluded, "Sex offenders who lived within closer proximity to schools and daycare centers did not re-offend more frequently than those who lived farther away. The time that police and probation officers spend addressing housing issues is likely to divert law enforcement resources away from behaviors that truly threaten our communities in order to attend to a problem that simply does not exist."[20]

Although these incidences are unusual, perhaps the media coverage on the abduction, rape, and killing of children causes such a stir that leads the public to overestimate how widespread

---

19 http://i.usatoday.net/news/pdf/Pew%20Center%20on%20the%20States,%20PSPP%20Recidivism%20Report.pdf
20 http://lubbockonline.com/interact/blog-post/josie-musico/2015-01-29/sex-offender-residency-restrictions-what-does-research#.VoRc9Vnhbct

these cases really are. The mass media can give the public a warped sense of life's hazards.[21]

Reasons Behind the Hysteria

There are several reasons for hysteria and dread encompassing predator panic.

News stories accentuate the risks of Internet predators, offenders convicted of sexual malpractices, pedophiles, and child kidnappings. The Today Show, for instance, ran a series of deceiving and concealed camera "tests" to check whether outsiders would offer a kidnapped child some assistance. Dateline NBC collaborated with a group called Perverted Justice to draw potential online predators to a house with shrouded cameras. The system's appraisals were high to the point that it brought forth six preliminary "To Catch a Predator" specials. While the numerous men captured on film to meet teenagers for sex is exasperating, questions have been raised about Perverted Justice's techniques and accuracy. (For instance, the predators are regularly found in unmoderated chatrooms frequented by those searching for casual sex - barely in places where most kids spend their time).

It is also amazing that out of over a hundred million Internet clients, a small percentage may be found in such a sting. Since there is minimal practical information on how prevalent the issue of Internet predators is, writers frequently depend on emotionalism, cobbling a couple of stories and interviews together into a pattern while sparkling over information proposing that the issue may not be as far-reaching as they claim. Great news coverage requires that individual stories - regardless of how enthusiastic and convincing - must be modified to certainties and context. A significant part of the

---

21   http://archive.wilsonquarterly.com/in-essence/fearful-confusion

news scope about sexual predation is less wrong but rather more fragmented, the lacking point of view.

Moral Fears

The news media's inclination toward alarmism somehow clarifies the worry. America, for a long time, has been in the hold of moral fears over sexual predators. A moral fear is a sociological term depicting a social response to a false or overstated danger to social qualities by moral nonconformists. In a discussion of ethical fears, Robert Bartholomew, a sociologist, states that a marking feature of the fear is that the "Worry about the risk postured by moral aliens and their numerical magnitude is far more prominent than can be impartially confirmed, notwithstanding unverified cases to the contrary." Furthermore, as per Goode and Ben-Yehuda, amid moral fears "The vast majority of the figures referred to by moral fear claims-makers' are uncontrollably misrepresented."[22]

In fact, we see precisely this pattern in the fear of sexual predators. News stories constantly overstate the genuine degree of sexual predation on the Internet; the extent of the threat to kids, and the probability that sexual predator will strike. Attorney General Gonzales (2005-2007) had taken his 50,000 Web figures not from any governmental report or research, but rather from NBC's Dateline TV show. Dateline, thusly, had telecast the number a few times without checking its precision. In a meeting on NPR's On the Media program, Hansen conceded that he had the source for the figures, and expressed that "It was credited to, law requirement, as an evaluation, and it was discussed as kind of an extrapolated number." According to Wall Street Journal essayist Carl Bialik, columnists "Regularly will utilize questionable numbers to propel that objective [of shielding children] . . . A reason this is permitted to happen is

---

22 Ehrich Goode and Nachman Ben-Yehuda's 1994 book *Moral Panics: The Social Construction of Deviance.*

that there isn't a characteristic pundit. No one truly needs to go on the record saying, "It turns out this truly isn't a major issue."

Apprehensive Laws

Other than unnecessarily terrifying children and people in general, there is a peril to this kind of reportage: deceiving news stories impact officials, who thusly respond with honest (and voter-friendly) moral shock. Since almost any measure expected (or guaranteed) to secure kids will be well received and unopposed, lawmakers stumble over themselves in the hurry to embrace new laws that "shield the children." Government officials, kid advocates, and writers condemn current laws against sex offenders as insufficient and imperfect, yet are seldom ready to express precisely why new laws are required. Rather, they refer to every news anecdote around a hijacked youngster or Web predator as evidence that more laws are required, as though sex violations would stop if the current punishments were harsher, or enough individuals were checked. The way that uncommon wrongdoings keep on being perpetrated does not as a matter, of course, infer that present laws against those violations are deficient. By that standard, any law is ineffectual if somebody abuses that law. We don't accept that current laws against homicide are inadequate just in light of the fact that murders keep on being conferred.

In July 2006, abduction victim, Elizabeth Smart and children activist John Walsh (whose murdered son Adam brought forth America's Most Wanted) were instrumental in passing the broadest national sex offender bill ever. As indicated by Senator Orrin Hatch (R-Utah), the bill's supporter, Smart's 2002 "Kidnapping by a sentenced sex offender" may have been averted had his bill been law. "I would prefer not to see others experience what I went through," said Smart. "This bill ought to be passed without a second thought." Bills that went without thought occasionally make great laws. A critical look at the instances of Elizabeth Smart and Adam Walsh exhibit why sex crime registries don't secure youngsters. Like the majority who abducted kids like, David Mitchell, had never been previously charged with sex crimes nor was Adam Walsh snatched by a sex offender. Evidently not able to locate a vocal advocate for a minor who had been snatched by a known sex offender, Hatch utilized Smart and Walsh to advance a plan that had nothing to do with the circumstances of their kidnappings. The two prominent abductions (neither by previously indicted sex offenders) were some way or another guaranteed to exhibit the earnest requirement for more tightly confinements on those guilty of sex crimes. For this reason, Hatch's 2006 bill will probably have little impact in ensuring the safety of America's kids.

The last prominent government push to thwart Internet predation took place in December 2002, when President Bush marked the Dot-Kids Implementation and Efficiency Act into law, an effort to make an especially secure Internet "neighborhood" for minors. Elliot Noss, President of Internet Location Enlistment Center Tucows Inc., accurately foretold that the domain had "totally zero" probability of being viable. The ".kids.us" space is presently a disregarded Internet footnote that has done little or nothing to secure kids.

Tragically Misleading

The issue is not whether youngsters should be shielded; obviously, they do. The issues are whether the risk to them is large and whether the measures proposed will guarantee their well-being. While a few endeavors, for example, longer sentences for repeat sex crimes by known offenders - are all around contemplated and prone to be powerful, those centered around isolating people with sexual offenses from the general population are of little worth because they depend on a defective reason. Mainly knowing where a discharged registered offender lives - or is at any given minute - does not guarantee that he or she won't be close to a potential victim. Since a low number of sexual attacks are perpetrated by known sex offenders, the worry over the peril is uncontrollably unbalanced to the genuine danger. All the same, endeavors to secure kids have positive intentions, however, enactment ought to be founded on certainties and valid arguments rather than a national moral fear.

The tragically misleading fear over registered sex offenders diverts the general population from the genuine peril, a far more prominent risk to youngsters than sexual predators: parental/guardian/caregiver neglect and/or abuse. Most by far of violations against youngsters are submitted not by people with prior sex offenses but rather by the victim's family, church ministry, and family companions. As per a 2003 report by the Department of Human Services[23], a huge number of youngsters are mishandled and neglected every year by their guardians and parental figures, and more than 1,500 American kids were killed from that manhandle in 2003 - the majority of the casualties under four years of age. That is more than four minors killed every day - not by indicted sexual guilty parties or Internet predators, but rather by those endowed to watch over them. The real danger to children is greater from someone they or their family knows than from a stranger. Seeing as "most sexual abuse offenders are acquainted with their victims; approximately 30% are relatives of the child, most often brothers, fathers, uncles, or cousins; around 60% are other acquaintances, such as "friends" of the family, babysitters, or neighbors; strangers are the offenders in approximately 10% of child sexual abuse cases."[24]

If child advocates, lawmakers, journalists, and officials are determined on protecting the children, they ought to tackle the real issue; and channel the funds assigned to following

---

23   http://archive.acf.hhs.gov/programs/cb/pubs/cm03/cm2003.pdf
24   Julia Whealin, Ph.D. (2007-05-22). "Child Sexual Abuse". National Center for Post-Traumatic Stress Disorder, US Department of Veterans Affairs.

ex-criminals who are not likely to repeat the crime towards preventing child abuse in the home.[25]

Dealing With F.E.A.R

"A lie told often enough becomes the truth," said Vladimir Lenin. Clearly when that happens people begin to make decisions under F.E.A.R:

False
Evidence
Appearing
Real

Where false evidence, rather than genuine facts is employed, the real picture is distorted. Instead of fanning the hysteria around sex offenders in the church and the public at large, the church ought to teach youngsters from an early age to know precisely what to do if somebody tries to exploit them. We are to present truth to them according to their age and level of understanding. Without causing fear and unfounded suspicion, minors should be informed that sexual predators are incredibly deceitful; and can disguise as preachers, mentors or church counselors.

Stories such as Ammon's manipulation of circumstances to get alone with a trusting sister and after exploiting her sexually (2 Samuel 13), should be re-done (without changing the Biblical meaning) in a way that can communicate the truth to potential victims. They should be encouraged to shout for help in the face of such danger; that's well in line with Deuteronomy 22:23-24.

Generally, many casualties of sexual offenses are naive and defenseless. The church comes in to mirror God's specific care for the powerless and the abused (Proverbs 31:8-9) It's interesting that God defends the cause of the oppressed

---

[25] http://www.csicop.org/si/show/predator_panic_a_closer_look/

(victim) and sets the prisoner (sex offender) free (Psalm 146:7). Therefore, even as Christians assume liability to help and assure victims while uncovering any questionable sexual behavior by leaders against minors in our midst, we should be aware that the church has a dual responsibility. Church leaders who abuse their position of power and leadership must be openly dealt with (1 Timothy 5:19-20) and, where appropriate, their violations must be accounted for to the administration powers (Romans 13:1ff). Spiritual leaders who exploit others sexually should be disqualified permanently from authority (1 Timothy 3:1-7) regardless of how skilled or powerful they might appear to be. The Bible also warns us of the consequences of sexual immorality. The church ought also to convey the reality of the consequences of un-repented sexual offenses (Jude 1:7).

Part 2

The Impairment: Dealing with the residual effects of the issue regarding the growth of the ministry and the individual

4

When Sex Offenders Attend Church

Social support is a crucial element in a convicted sex offender's reintegration into the community;[26] yet, many have lost the social support of family and friends. They turn to churches for the social support they require. Thus, some clergy and churches have become a social support for sex offenders, but some do so devoid of the expertise necessary to understand the motivational and cognitive-behavioral aspects of sexual offenses or how to handle conflicts that can crop up when a sex offender attends church or becomes a member.[27]

Conversely, operating a church while under the influence of hysteria impairs the vision of the church, while its lingering effects hamper the development of both the church and the person. If we, the church is in panic of predators, how will they be reached?

"How, then, can they call on the one they have not believed in? And how can they believe in the one of whom they have not heard? And how can they hear without someone preaching to them?" Romans 10:4 NIV

This seems to imply that, if we expect the person to turn over a new leaf they have to be led - and who else better to offer this leadership than the church? I once heard that the only Jesus some people will ever meet in their lifetime is you (the Christian).

Traditionally, churches are known to be places of refuge - and in many cases, wherever a church is in operation, the presence of children and other vulnerable groups are inevitable. There is fear when a known sex offender is in the midst. We ask, "Should they be here?" If we allow them, won't we be risking

---

26 W. R. Lindsay et al., "Self-Regulation of Sex Offending, Future Pathways and the Good Lives Model: Applications and Problems," Journal of Sexual Aggression 13, no. 1 (2007): 37–50.
27 https://www.ministrymagazine.org/archive/2013/09/sex-offenders-in-the-church

the welfare of our children; and if we don't let them in, won't we be violating their constitutional and biblical right to worship?

Many neighborhoods have come up with association policies excluding offenders from living there. Now more and more churches are hoping onto the wagon - adopting a secular view in dealing with registered sex offenders. While making efforts to extend a welcome to the registered sex offenders, they protectively drape a cloak of safety over the children and others in the next pew.

Balancing the needs of people who are attempting to get spiritual guidance and the safety of a congregation is a difficult issue.

The Crime Scene Kansas City site shares some thought-provoking comments. One commenter makes the very salient point that "sex offender," as currently interpreted, can take on different meanings, from an 18-year-old teenager sleeping with a slightly younger partner to - in very seldom cases - public urination. As such, it requires any such congregation to look into the accusation and record of any such known sex offender.

One man who has been a registered sex offender for a decade said that he found compassion in his church. "I am Roman Catholic and I have followed my own personal restrictions. I attend early morning mass (very few children at 7:00am). I avoid going to activities where there are children. This is not imposed by my parish, but this is my decision to avoid any problems and protect the church. We are all sinners and by coming to terms with our sinfulness through giving our lives to God, Jesus... is when we will find peace and forgiveness."[28]

---

28 http://blogs.kansascity.com/crime_scene/2010/08/should-churches-welcome-sex-offenders.html,
http://jezebel.com/5602474/how-sex-offenders-go-to-church

From Indifference to Action

Since not every individual who commits a sexual offense is convicted or adjudicated, victims should be encouraged to report any allegations. Gone are the days when sexual offenses within the church were swept under the rug, to the detriment of the victims. We have evolved from silence to action. In her book Trauma and Recovery,[29] author Judith Herman writes, "It is very tempting to take the side of the perpetrator. All the perpetrator asks is that the bystander do nothing. He appeals to the universal desire to see, hear, and speak no evil. The victim, on the contrary, asks the bystander to share the burden of pain. The victim demands action, engagement, and remembering."

While the church can play an important social and spiritual role in helping a sex offender avoid the risk of re-offending, the role of the church in ministering to these individuals must be moderated by the needs of victims and the safety of the congregation.

As Christians (the church of Jesus Christ), we know that our sins can be forgiven and washed away, but their consequences are ours to pay. Therefore, in taking action and generating limitations, the sex offender must understand that the church is not against them.

---

29 Judith Herman, *Trauma and Recovery* (New York: Basic Books, 1992), 7, 8.

5
Residual Damage

A story is told of a young teenage boy who continuously got into trouble and always apologized whenever confronted by his parents. Regardless of how much he hurt his parents with his earlier bad behavior, he would soon turn around and do something else erroneous - fully aware that he would be forgiven.

Eventually, his daddy took him out to the garage for a talk. The older man picked up a hammer and hit a nail into the garage wall. Then handed the hammer to his son and instructed him to pull out the nail.

Shrugging, the boy grabbed the hammer, and yank out the nail.

"That's like forgiveness, Son." Said Dad. "When you do something wrong, it's like pounding in a nail;" he continued, "forgiveness is when you pull the nail out."

"Okay, I get it," said the lad.

"Now use the hammer to yank out the nail hole," came his dad's reply.

"That's not possible!" the boy said. "I can't pull the nail hole out."

Moral of the story: Sin carries consequences. Remember King David's fall from grace?[30] As his life proves, although he was forgiven, his adultery and murder left blemishes and led to family problems.

"Now, therefore, the sword will never depart from your house, because you despised me and took the wife of Uriah the Hittite to be your own.' "This is what the Lord says: 'Out of your own household I am going to bring calamity on you. Before your very eyes I will take your wives and give them to one who is close to you,

---

30 2 Samuel 11:1-27

and he will sleep with your wives in broad daylight. You did it in secret, but I will do this thing in broad daylight before all Israel. But because by doing this you have shown utter contempt for the Lord, the son born to you will die." 2 Samuel 12:10-11, 14 NIV

What a sobering truth! It can serve as a warning for our lives. The surest way to avoid the residual damage of offense is to live a life of obedience to God - in so doing, we'll not rouse hysteria in our neighbors.

Sex Offenders in Church: To Ban or Not to Ban?

The Bible Belt of the United States, of which North Carolina is a member, takes its faith seriously. Therefore, when James Nichols was taken into custody for attending church, it came as a surprise to many.

Despite being a convicted sex offender, Nichols had decided to worship at a church, where while parents prayed, kids played in the nursery. Being present there was his crime.

By October 2009, Nichols was 31 and had just been released from prison. He took up the battle of challenging the legitimacy of a new law that had been affected the previous December barring registered sex offenders from coming within 300 feet - about the length of a football field - of any location dedicated to the use, care and or supervision of minors.

In dealing with residual effects of the issue at hand in regard to the growth of the ministry and the individual, the question arises - Should registered sex offenders be prohibited from church? Although there is crucial need to protect our children, with increased states adopting laws to regulate where sex offenders can attend worship, there is a definite likelihood of interfering with the First Amendment right to worship where and when one chooses. What's our priority?

Nichols' lawyer, Glen Gerding, said that this particular law[31] renders it illegal to do things that are right, like go to church. He questioned whether a pastor would be charged as an accessory for allowing a registered sex offender to attend worship; wondering when the state would stop interfering with a church's business.

While North Carolina's law is somewhat less strict, it is still a fact that most states limit sex offenders' movements in one way or another. In Georgia, a known sex offender is required to stay away 1,000 feet of places with minors. Their courts ruled in support of the right of offenders to participate in activities, as well as volunteer in church kitchens, go to adult Sunday school and sing in the church choir.

Southern Center for Human Rights, an Atlanta-based organization sued the state over its residency and employment limitations, along with prohibiting faith-based volunteering. Besides running in contradiction to the church's mission of inclusion, hospitality and redemption, banning someone from attending church presents grave constitutional problems.

The moment North Carolina's law took effect, the state's American Civil Liberties Union (ACLU) chapter, began receiving calls. On one hand, offenders wanted to find out if the regulation prohibited them from going to church; on the other, clergymen were concerned that it would keep parishioners away. Isn't it mind-boggling to keep a person from attending church for both spiritual and rehabilitative reasons? Yet, should a known sex offender go into a church, donning a cloak of protection from the rule of law? Wouldn't that, then, make churches sanctuaries for crime?

At the age of 20, Nichols was convicted of indecent liberties with a teenage girl and attempted second-degree rape. After

---

31   The law is named for Jessica Lunsford, the Florida girl who was kidnapped and killed in 2005 by a convicted sex offender.

his release, he had attended North Carolina's Moncure Baptist Church for several months ahead of the police paying any attention. What is strange is that he (Nichols) unintentionally 'revealed' himself when he alerted law enforcement regarding a fellow congregant (another lawbreaker), whom he observed fondling a 12-year-old girl.

When you think you are doing what's correct and instead, receive what is evidently a punishment for your past, giving up on God can be very easy. Nichols, however, recognizes that faith has kept him out of trouble. His before-prison sporadic church attendance was not sufficient, now he goes to New Life Mission Church in Fayetteville, N.C., practically every day. The church has no nursery on site and no children in their services.

The church should be a place that allows rehabilitation, regardless of someone's background. David Hoyle, the state senator who sponsored the bill, that took two years to pass, says, "When a person takes advantage of a child, I don't worry about their constitutional rights."[32] In this breath, there is utterly no room for grace.

---

32 http://content.time.com/time/nation/article/0,8599,1929736,00.html

6

Where is Grace?

If you have attended church, even intermittently, you must have heard something about grace. Sermon and teachings on the need to forgive sin, treat each other with love, and scores of other akin biblical concepts go out every week. The church is a place where those concepts are modeled. Nonetheless, practically implementing those ideas into our not-so-perfect world is a lot easier said than done. Specifically, many churches battle with the issue of dealing with known criminals, particularly convicted sex offenders, who come to church and intermingle with the regular congregation, attend programs and seek to volunteer. If churches do not extend some grace then their ministry to such individuals will be non-existent. In the next chapter, we will discuss what I call The Resolve. We address several ways the church can come to a place of repentance, love and acceptance of societies most despised; and how to minister to them. But now let's look at the boundaries which the church can set in dealing with residual effects of hysteria against sex offenders.

Biblical View

We are aware that many churches have come face to face with this issue and there have been a variety of reactions. Some churches have put into effect a strict, no-tolerance stand and will not consent to sexual offenders coming onto church grounds or becoming members. On the opposite side of the scale, many churches seem to have not contemplated on the issue and have no clear helpful way to handle convicted sex offenders or criminals.

What does the Bible suggest? To get biblical recommendations we have to look at similar situations. In our day, sexual offenses are viewed as leprosy[33] and the perpetrators, "modern-day lepers". During Biblical times, this disease was looked upon as a dreadful punishment from God (2 Kings 5:7; 2 Chronicles 26:20); and its sufferers were required to reside outside the camp or town (Numbers 5:1-4; 12:10-15). They were not permitted to live in a walled city, although an open (un-walled) community would be fine. However, wherever a leper was it was mandatory that they should have their outer garment torn as a sign of intense sorrow, their head uncovered, and beard covered with his mantle, as if in lamentation at their own virtual death. Besides that, they had to call out, "Unclean! Unclean!" - A caution to passersby to stay clear from them. Furthermore, the lepers weren't allowed to speak to anyone or receive or return a greeting, because according to the Eastern traditions this action requires both the giver and recipient to embrace.

Leviticus 13:12, 13, 36; and 2 Kings 5:1 seem to debunk the notion that leprosy was contagious, rather the scriptures uphold that the disease was the external and evident sign of the secret spiritual decadence; which begins as small specks but gradually spreads to disfigure the whole body, rendering the sufferer unfit to go into the presence of a pure and holy God.

We are in the grace era, so whether or not the disease is contagious is not the issue; our concern is how to handle the disease. Here, the term "disease" (dis-ease) will refer to the issue as "disabling the ease of the people". How did Jesus handle dis-

---

33   Also known as **Hansen's disease (HD)**, is a chronic infection caused by the bacteria *Mycobacterium leprae* and *Mycobacterium lepromatosis*. Initially, infections are without symptoms and typically remain this way from 5 to as long as 20 years. Symptoms that develop include granulomas of the nerves, respiratory tract, skin, and eyes. This may result in a lack of ability to feel pain and thus loss of parts of extremities due to repeated injuries or infection due to unnoticed wounds. Weakness and poor eyesight may also be present. Leprosy is spread between people. It is believed to occur through a cough or contact with fluid from the nose of an infected person. Leprosy occurs more commonly among those living in poverty and is believed to be transmitted by respiratory droplets. Contrary to popular belief, it is not very contagious and is curable with a treatment known as multidrug therapy (MDT).

eases? He cured them - period! Who is the church expected to emulate? Jesus! Our Lord graciously cured lepers (Matthew 8:2, 3; Mark 1:40-42). When a sexual offender comes to the church, it means that there is a part of him that is seeking to be forgiven and set free. Although small, this part is like a seed that should be nurtured.

"Therefore, my friends, I want you to know that through Jesus the forgiveness of sins is proclaimed to you. Through him everyone who believes is set free from every sin, a justification you were not able to obtain under the law of Moses." Acts 13:38-39 NIV

We, the church ought not to chain the offenders to their past sins. The church should possess the divine power of God in order to manifest the ability to practically illustrate Christ's gracious dealings with perpetrators of sexual crimes (or any other sin) in curing this leprosy of the soul!

Grace doesn't shut you out, nor does it discriminate; it embraces you as you are, but refuses to leave you the same. Grace offers a helping hand while creating an avenue for change - even to whom it formerly didn't exist (and all the Gentiles, said amen!).

"For the grace of God has appeared that offers salvation to all people. It teaches us to say "No" to ungodliness and worldly passions, and to live self-controlled, upright and godly lives in this present age." Titus 2:11-12 NIV

Clear teachings of what the true church of Jesus Christ stands for will illuminate the congregants' understanding of grace and forgiveness. When grace is extended to a genuinely repentant offender, he/she receives the power to live a self-controlled life and the members will be relieved of fear.

'For God hath not given us the spirit of fear; but of power, and of love, and of a sound mind." 2 Timothy 1:7 KJV

Secularism[34] has its way of imposing restrictions in an attempt to provide a solution, but the church has an obligation to stick by the Word. In so doing churches should be able to mold a solution relevant to their members' concerns and wishes, allowing for effective ministry, and that honors God.

For both the ministry and the individuals to experience positive growth, the church must not shy away from dealing with the embers of exaggerated panic around sex offenders in the pews. One congregant getting hysterical over the presence of a previously convicted criminal can easily cause others to panic, further worsening the situation. For that reason, the church's implementation of a holistic approach to the Scriptures will help both the person in question and the questioning to party receive ministry.

---

34   Belief system that rejects religion, or the belief that religion should not be part of the affairs of the state or part of public education. The principles of separation of church and state and of keeping religion out of the public school system is an example of secularism.

Part 3

The Resolve: Helping the church come to a place of repentance, love, and acceptance

7

How Are Churches Ministering to Society's Most Despised?

A teenage girl walking down the hallways at school thinking that if they lost at least fifteen pounds they would look as attractive as the other girls and have guys swooning over her. To her, it matters very little that the doctor said she was healthy and her weight was where she should be. Sitting down at her desk, she is thinking that if she were a little smarter, she'd have near to a 100% in her advanced classes, than she already had. She wears makeup because she thinks her skin is ugly and that peers would mock her. If only she would fit in!

That is just an example of someone (not necessarily an offender) struggling with something. To them, it is like a disease that has a hidden cure which seems impossible to find. Such a person is eager for a new chapter - a place of acceptance - in their life. Such is the case of the known sex offender - he/she seeks that place, somewhere they can go to express their repentance, and receive love along with acceptance. The general public looks down on them, but the church is called to live by a higher standard.

> *"Do not conform to the pattern of this world, but be transformed by the renewing of your mind. Then you will be able to test and approve what God's will is - his good, pleasing and perfect will."* Romans 12:2 NIV

How can we know God's perfect will if we operate the same way the world does? How Are Churches Ministering to Society's Most Despised?

"By ministering to them, it's not necessarily saying, we trust you...it does say that within Christ, we have hope for you." Religious institutions, by their nature, do operate under a different system, for example, Bernie Madoff's synagogue felt compelled to make it clear that they'd accept a registered sex offender as a congregant and this after he had defrauded not only half the congregation but the institution itself. Forgiveness, as they say, is divine - even when it goes against the human part.[35]

Committing non-consensual sexual relations, especially with minors is a crime that earns one the title of sex offender. Craig, for example, an anonymous sex offender who was serving a sentence for sexual assault and abuse against his young daughter and another girl had wondered if the church had a place for him. According to Anglican Theologian N.T Wright, every society has that one unforgivable sin - was Craig's the one? When the prison chaplain asked Craig if he would want to accept Jesus, he replied if Jesus would want to accept him because of this sin.

Life After Prison

Craig was serving in a local church and got support for his recovery in lust addiction. He was a volunteer for a sex addiction ministry. In September 2010, he and

his family were changing churches and he had made an appointment with the church pastor to discuss his past. This was essential for him being aware that rejection was

part of the consequence of his sin even as he awaited the verdict.

Going Beyond the Risk Involved

Pastors, church leaders, and the congregation all believe that once the sex offenders serve their sentence, they should be welcomed into the church and the society. Speaking about the unpardonable sin, Jesus, in the Gospel of Matthew, said, *"And so I tell you, every kind of sin and slander can be forgiven, but blasphemy against the Spirit will not be forgiven." Matthew 12:31 NIV*

---

[35] http://jezebel.com/5602474/how-sex-offenders-go-to-church

So then, to minister effectively, sex offenders too should be forgiven and not judged. After all, who are we to cast stones?[36]

However, this doesn't mean the church wants to condone sexual crimes, but it should provide a safe environment - a place of refuge where people from all walks of life can come because they sense the presence of Christ's protection. Parents wouldn't have to fear for their children and people with a sexual conviction can breathe a sigh of relief for not being judged. That is the prayer of Mark Tusken, St. Mark's Church in Geneva, Illinois who says that in his 16 years as the congregation's overseer, he has known of only one convicted sex offender attending.

It is a great challenge for the church to accept the sex offenders and mainly because the congregation thinks they are outcasts, but it is a wonderful challenge to make a difference in the society. Getting to know the sex offender and accepting him/her in the church by the leadership is an effective way to ensure that they feel welcome and can help them open up to talk about their sins and how to rectify them. This can be a great healing on their part, which shows progress and acceptance that they made a mistake and are willing to turn over a new leaf.

Trust and Verification Go Hand in Hand

Anna Salter, a clinical psychologist consultant on sex offenders and victims cautions in her 2003 book "Predators: Pedophiles, Rapists, and other Sex Offenders". She reports that many sex offenders perceive church goers as being the easiest to deceive since they are Christians and want to believe in people - a trust that comes from their Christian faith. Church leaders want their lives to exemplify what Jesus said in John 8:12, *"I am the light of the world. Whoever follows me will never walk in darkness, but will have the light of life."*

---

36 John 8:7

They would like to bring light into the dark spaces of the offenders' hearts and the hurting heart of their victims. Trust alone is not enough, ministers should take extra precautions to prevent such cases from happening again. They should implement safety policies such as having all adults in key positions in the church go through child protection training programs. Systems like that can work if we truly believe that just as an alcoholic or drug addict can change, sex offenders can change, too.

For effective ministry to persons with a sexual offense, cooperation from them is extremely mandatory. A covenant agreement with the offender is created stating what their offense was, and how church officials feel they are doing in their journey toward recovery. Decisions may be based on court rulings and the help of lay professionals in the church. Such lay professionals may include a social worker, a defense attorney, a criminal court advocate, psychologists and psychiatrists, or retired police officers.

The Road to Redemption

Churches are usually one of the parties in the re-entry and prevention programs for these offenders and yet we see churches that fall or close down simply because the congregation is unable to handle the presence of the sex offenders. Besides the church being devoid of good working models, programs geared towards redemption of sex offenders may fail because of the negative environment that has been created in how we perceive sex offenders.

Case in point

Don Bryant, a former pastor of a small congregation outside Boston, has his theories too. "In my 30-plus years as a minister, I have never asked someone to leave the church because their redemptive process was too messy. But what I learned in trying to work with a sex offender at our church is that you need more of a critical mass of people invested in recovery as a ministry."

With only about 75 members in his congregation, Bryant said there were just not enough people to sustain the level of care and attention the sex offender's presence required.

When the church dwindled to 35 people, Bryant went to his church board and suggested they close their doors. Although those who left the church never admitted it, Bryant sensed a diminished energy among them for having to deal with the offender.

"The sex offender is the broken and bruised man," says ex-offender Craig. "He is isolated by the nature of his crimes. To come alongside and reflect Christ through accountability and assistance, to offer mentorship—these would be the most helpful things a church could do. But most churches don't even want to talk about sex, much less sex offenses. And yet to have someone to talk to honestly and openly about their struggles - that's what being a Christian is all about."

Another reason many churches don't have recovery programs may be that they simply do not have a working model. But one group may have cracked the code.[37]

---

37 http://www.christianitytoday.com/ct/2010/september/21.49.html

8

Hostility Towards Sex Offenders: Brief History

As early as the 1690s, sexual offenders were being hanged and killed. In Salem, for example, witches, who were considered sex offenders for consulting with the evil spirits, were hanged and crushed under heavy stone. Social unrest and high rates of unemployment followed due to the many riots and the rise of great dictators like Hitler and Stalin. These acts of terrorism have made people look for ways to seek vengeance and the need to feel safe. Today, the terror threat has made many nations watch as Iran and North Korea gain the power which can trigger a war in order to put an end to the terrorist activity going on in the world today. We thus need to feel safe and secure and this leads to the sex offenders being registered as terrorists and their personal information is available all over the internet.

Sex offenders are usually supposed to visit the police station every four months, failure to which earns them a new penalty to be charged with. In some states they are not supposed to live near schools, bus stations or even near day care centers and any violation makes them guilty and punishable by law. They are treated differently from other people since we see them being given different licenses. Whenever a sex offender moves into a new neighborhood, all the neighbors are usually notified. The neighbors can evict them or the neighbors even with the use of violence.

Specific Incidences of Violence Against Sex Offenders

Lawrence Trant, from Concord, NH, is seen stabbing a sex offender and attempted to burn down two apartments where about seven sex offenders live with other non-sex offenders. In an interview while in prison, he is seen saying that he hopes he has done the community a huge favor since sex offenders are sexual terrorists.

Three years after the Trant case, a mob is seen burning a scarecrow in front of the house porch of Gloria Huot, who is also a sex offender. Her roommate experienced the whole thing since Huot was at home in Manchester. Days later, a sex offender's vigilante website leaves a statement saying that sex offenders should be punished for the rest of their lives and a bit of harassment is leniency to them.

We also see Stephen Marshall from Nova Scotia executing two registered sex offenders in Maine in 2006 before killing himself on a bus in Massachusetts when surrounded by the police. Just like Trant, he also found his victims on the Internet registry.

All these examples are proof of just how much we despise the sex offenders and people are willing to kill them just to save the community from their bad activities. This is contrary to the sixth commandment in the bible which forbids anyone from committing murder. The same is in Luke 6:37 which forbids anyone from judging and they too shall not be judged.

There is Hope Even (Especially) For the Sex Offender

Despite the entire evil manner in which the public has reacted towards the sex offenders, and also the poor judgment we put on them, there is still hope for the people with sex offenses to improve their environment once they get out of prison. Canada keeps a non-public sex offender registry for the police when they need to solve crimes. They also do well to help sex offenders find jobs, places to live and a working support system once they get out. The Mennonites in Canada arguably make sure that the sex offenders are rehabilitated and mentored in the most effective way especially the more dangerous sex offenders. Their program model is called Circles of Support and Accountability. It serves the kind of people in California and Kansas and would civilly commit after they finish their prison terms.

The Circles program usually helps the sex offenders understand the great harm they have caused and help learn ways to repair that harm. The recovery process is either directed to their victim or directed in them living safely in the community, by changing the choices made and by doing community service.[38]

---

38 http://www.corrections.com/news/article/30086-there-s-hope-even-for-sex-offenders

9

The Role of the Church

The church is one of the great avenues to help the sex offenders once they get out of prison. This is because it is a neutral setting that has the characteristics of forming programs to help the vulnerable people in society. If truth be told, sex offenders are never treated well while in prison since they are the lowest of all people due to their crimes. When they get out of prison, they are treated harshly by society. Their names are put on a sex offender registry and accessible from the internet for the rest of their lives. Thus, the church is a good avenue for the sex offenders to find shelter and comfort especially in their first year outside bars - since this is the most difficult time for them.

However, many are the times we see the church doing in contrary of what is expected of them. The congregation itself can even shift from a church that has welcomed the sex offenders for many reasons including security. Moreover, many churches usually refuse to accept them for moral reasons, publicity, and the fear of losing their church members. This has made many sex offenders feel unwelcome by the one thing that can save them from their agony.

To rectify this situation, the church must step up and face this great challenge and accept the sex offender because they are also human beings. There are many recommendations which are laid down for the church to enable them to accommodate the sex offender in the church. (You may refer to the subheading "Imposed Restrictions" in the preceding chapter) In addition to ministering to the person, these restrictions exist to ensure the safety of the congregation. The sex offender can be assigned someone who can help prevent the sex offender from falling into temptation again. Since the purpose of the church program is to ensure that the sex offenders have succeeded, there is also the need to introduce counseling sessions which will make sure that they progress. The sessions can be conducted by the pastor, a church leader, or a professional counselor. These methods are great for the sex offenders in their journey towards freedom and redemption.

However, in as much as the church needs to take precaution for the safety of the congregation, showing trust can be a good thing for the sex offenders. Giving them the love and support are essential tools to boost their self-esteem and feel the need to make efforts to improve. The church has the responsibility of preaching love, acceptance, and forgiveness to the congregation so that they can learn that these are important tools to the sex offender. The congregation needs to treat them in a better way so that they can feel they are loved and needed back in the society - this will give them new hope. With this kind of approach, the sex offender will have no reason to feel rejected and possibly go back to their sinful life.

After the program, the church should let the sex offender remain in the church and get to know Christ. This is, however, to those who are willing to do so. They should be forgiven and led to say a prayer of salvation so that they can get saved and form a relationship with Christ. Doing so will help them develop better relationships with other people and improve their life skills. They should be incorporated in church activities to keep them busy and occupied. In this way, they will feel welcome and accepted by the community in ways we can never understand.

Therefore, the church has a great role to play for the re-entry of the sex offenders back into the society to be successful. The church needs to be loving and accepting towards sex offenders, as well as accepting repentance from them. Just like other sinners are forgiven, sex offenders are no exception. Once they repent, they need to be trusted and loved for their efforts to change to be successful. If the church fails to do this then they make Jesus death on the cross discriminatory. Christ died on that cross for the redemption of each person, including sex offenders. They should not live in condemnation for the rest of their lives due to their sins. The church has the greatest job to ensure that all goes well with them. We, the church, should end the judgment and criticism against people with sex offenses - just because they sinned differently than we did. We have an opportunity to embrace and an obligation to repent for missing it. Since the church is one of the greatest avenues for reforming the sex offenders, it should have the best programs and acceptance mechanisms to allow the sex offenders to feel secure and safe under its wing.

Watchful Grace:
Answerability for Sex Offenders in the Congregation

We have already established that churches play a vital role in the reformation of offenders; convicted or not. It is in the church that every person is viewed as an equal (Galatians3:26-29) where they are part of the one body which is Christ's (Ephesians 2:14-16). Here, they can redeem themselves and have a chance of leading better lives. However, if the offender is an established threat to others, such as a sex offender, it is wise to extend a cautious and firm hand of help, rather than be polite and suffer retributions. Handling sex offenders are sensitive matters, and the church must maintain a neutral hand when doing so while giving ample attention to victims of sexual assault.

The church should be, and is, a player in rehabilitating/handling child sex offenders. Child sex abuse is among the most outrageous crime committed against children; ironically child pornography is a thriving industry. The concept is nothing surreal; it's recording of an individual defiling a child, committing a crime and not feeling sorry for it. Those who download and watch these clips or movies conceptually are like-minded with the perpetrators of the crimes they see. Crime against children is now recognized by many governments for what it is, a crime against the entire humanity. Jesus Christ teaches us that, whoever wishes to enter the kingdom of heaven should be like a little child; they are innocent and pure. Child pornography is a crime that takes away the innocence of a child. Jesus said that the person who lusts after a woman is a sinner similar to the one who commits the actual sin. Therefore, those who watch these acts are as good as the sinners themselves basing this on the fact that they enjoy watching the clips.

Researchers have continued to find evidence suggesting that a large portion of audience to child pornography often have committed or are charged with similar crimes. Therefore, despite the church's obligation to rehabilitate sexual offenders, it is everyone's best interest to remain cautious for the safety of the congregation. It is in this congregation that victims of sexual assault seek comfort, and still the same congregation is preyed upon by sex predators (Psalms 9:9). In the church, it is acknowledged that we are all sons and daughters of God, and therefore, we should not turn away anybody. Jesus walked and dined with sinners to demonstrate how the church should treat those who have sinned (Matthew 9:9-13). The work of the church is to help better those who have sinned and to take care of the vulnerable. Offenders are the sinners, and victims the weak; weakened by the assault and constant re-victimization through the distribution of their images and clips.

Sex offenders are part of the congregation when they come to church, and our call to the ministry is to share the Word with everybody. God's forgiveness transgresses all sins; sex offenders are sinners who too deserve a second chance in Christ (Ephesians 2:8). Romans 10:13 says that the key to salvation is calling upon the name of Lord and doing so saves one's life. The story of the prodigal son is a good example of how God cares for each one of us and is willing to forgive us if we repent. The Bible associates committing sin to acts of foolishness and relates wisdom to doing what is right (Proverbs 15:7). Clearly, it would be better to use careful grace when handling a scenario with a sex offender being part of the congregation.

Careful grace gives priority to victims and understands consequential results of decisions. Based on an understanding of offenders and their behavior when they interact with others allows responsible church officials to make wise decisions. It is in the same context that child and adult victims of sexual offenses are taken care off. The offenders are in the church to try and get well; it is, therefore, unwise to let them roam about with the rest of the congregation. The act is similar to releasing a wolf among sheep as described in Matthew 10:16.

Wisdom is important when deciding how the offenders will interact with the rest of the congregation. I'll reiterate here that a simple practice is having them sign a contract that explicitly states the borderline of their interactions with the rest of the congregation. Also, it should include strictly stated consequences applied when the guidelines are not adhered to. These contracts should bind offenders (all sexual related) indefinitely until further decisions are made by the church's officials. Such a practice demonstrates wisdom and allows such programs to succeed. The church should only engage in such programs when they are entirely suited to do so, that is, they are educated on children welfare and rehabilitation. Otherwise, they would be similar to Matthew 25:1-13 five foolish virgins who missed the bridegroom.

Those in the program should not be given trust roles in the public ministry as they may use the opportunity to lure more victims into trusting them. They are supposed to be assigned roles that help highlight their life changes. In some cases, before any offender is taken in, church officials should have an informed risk assessment from the person in charge of the offender. For instance, a probation officer, after which they can make an informed decision concerning the offender's continual desire to worship at their church or not.

Practices such as sharing should be restricted for the sex offenders, especially in public platforms; this is because different messages are sent out to the congregation. Children in the congregation might think that 'the person who could speak in the church must be a good person.' (Minors must be guided in truth. See "Dealing With F.E.A.R" in chapter 3). Like-minded parents might let their guard down on the basis that, the church must have found the offender safe enough. Also, victims in the congregation will feel unworthy and re-victimized by the offender's narration of crime, therefore affecting their healing process.

The survivors and others sharing strong resentment for these offenders will distant themselves from the church and may even leave completely. In graver circumstances, the church might be divided along the lines of supporting the decision and not supporting it; this destroys the purpose of a church. The church is one unified body and cannot be divided; if it is divided, it is not the body of Christ for there is one unified body (1 Corinthians1:10-17). In some unique cases, an offender might get sexually pleasured by merely talking about their life and the crimes they committed. For such talks, the church should hold private sessions with the offenders as they continue to help them change their lives.

The gospel of Christ is all about second chances that the Lord has granted all of us for we are all sinners. The only way to be cleansed is accepting our sins and repenting them. The sex offender's act of receiving rehabilitation sometimes is due to their deep-rooted hope of actually changing. Therefore, it is in our place as our brethren's watcher to cautiously guide them in the right direction (1 John 3:16). Furthermore, it is our duty not to cast away our sinful brethren, but to guide them back to gentleness and a good life (Galatians 6:1-2).

Are Sexual Sins Bigger Than God's Forgiveness?

According to what we have been taught and how we understand the concept of sin, we are declined to omit sexual sins in this category. Or sometimes assume it is in the et cetera placed at the end of the list if sins we know. Most people identify sin as insults, indulging in drugs or alcohol, but never draw their attention to the sexual subject. God is all-forgiving of all sins regardless of magnitude. You steal a pencil at school or rob a bank; you'll be forgiven when you ask. A sin is when a person does some action that they are aware of being wrong; this definition doesn't have boundaries. Perhaps the preachers and teachers find the topic too intimate or too personal to talk about, but it is happening every day of the week.

The Bible talks a lot about sex and in Deuteronomy 24, God gives the guidelines on how to not commit sexual sins. Therefore, there shouldn't be any refrain from preaching about it when it's a sin. Sex is how every child comes to be formed; it is the vital key to life God gave Adam and Eve to procreating their kind and fill the earth.

When does sin happen, and how does one get to do a wrong they are aware of? Satan after his downfall had decided to corrupt God's creation, he tempted Jesus after all. He is very calculating, he waits and finds a person's weakness then entices them to make that wrong move, and once you are in it, he is gone and returns to seduce you for more. Such a condition can be seen in offenders who act out then calm down the next moment.

Paul in I Corinthians 5:1 shows a resentful reaction but in 2 Corithians2:5-11, shows us the way God would like us to react; to comfort the one who has sinned, least they go back to doing wrong. Jesus mentioned that a person should forgive their brethren time after time provided they repent and for forgiveness (Luke 17:3-4). As good disciples, we should heed the words of Jesus, forgiving others and giving them a chance to change their behaviors. Above all else, we must realize that we are all bound by love; loving our neighbors as we do ourselves and loving God with everything we have (Timothy 1:7).

It is, therefore, our responsibility to look after each other; sex offenders and not forgetting the survivors in the church. Jesus forgave the woman who was going to be stoned by an angry mob (John 8:1-11); we should learn from this and continue being the light that shines on a hill for 'all' to seek refuge in. True ministry is taught through our lives; others look at how we live and how we interact to understand about what we teach. By preaching love, we should live lives that portray our love for each other as good neighbors. Jesus taught us about living a life of example, we should not preach water and drink wine. As we minister, we should reach out to those who are lost, just like the good shepherd who went searching for the one lost sheep.

Christ's Cross and Sex Offenders

Sexual offenders are among the most resented offenders since their crimes deeply harm the lives of survivors. Of these are child sex offenders, these are resented more, for children are considered as innocent and defenseless victims. Jesus suggests that causing a child to sin is graver sin than most others for He says that one who does so should be drowned (Matthew 18:6). Jesus said for a person to enter the kingdom of heaven, they should be like a child (Mark 10:14) implying that children are the best of all mankind.

The Bible teaches us to not to judge others for we too will be judged. We should accept all sinners and help them change their ways before being released back to the society. Jesus mentioned that His mission was not for the spiritually well, but for those who were ill; sinners who needed His help (Matthew 9:9-13). When He sent out His disciples, He told them to do

His work as He had taught them and cast out demons in His name (Luke 10:1). Today, we are the disciples, and we should be striving to emulate the life of Jesus. Therefore, we should try and guide our brethren in the right direction spiritually so that they can lead good lives. Our Lord directs us to love our neighbors as we love ourselves, and this does exclude sex offenders. By the way, how do you think Jesus (our Lord) would handle sex offenders?

To some extent, repentant sex offenders loosely relate their shame to the times of Jesus; lawbreakers often ended up shamefully crucified. It is clear that the wage of sin is death, but Jesus was crucified without sin so that no other sinner dies for their sins. Jesus' sacrifice was made especially for society's most despised.

10

Biblical Guiding Principles In Dealing With Sex Offenders

Understandably, sexual abuse and sex offenders are issues that are infused with emotion. For those who have abused the subject can cause a flood of emotions from fear to pain and shame. For others, disgust and anger. The church should be a safe place, yet Scripture warns us of wolves that come in (Acts 20:29), not sparing the flock and the devil, as a lion, is seeking for someone to consume (1 Peter 5: 8). Nevertheless, we should not respond to these dangers from a place of fear, rather, we should do so from the vantage point of submission to God. This submission calls for resisting the devil and doing things as God would have us do - like treat others as the Word teaches us to do. As Christians we are expected to take steps to protect the flock from danger, bind up the wounded and bring back those who have strayed (Ezekiel 34: 4, 34:22, Proverbs 22: 3). We are not to "be anxious about anything, but in everything by prayer and supplication with thanksgiving let our requests be made known to God" (Philippians 4:6). Whenever there is fear for doing the right thing we should remember that *"God gave us a spirit not of fear but of power and love and self-control" (2 Timothy 1:7)*. In spite of everything, when we respond with love, we will do away with fear because *"perfect love casts out fear. For fear has to do with punishment, and whoever fears has not been perfected in love" (1 John 4:18)*.

We Are All Sinners Saved By Grace

We must understand and accept that now the church will have people from all backgrounds, who are repentant, redeemed and reconciled with the Father, sex criminals in their ranks, as well. It is also reasonable to expect that some of them come to the church for a place to worship and grow. As we can see in the Scriptures, receiving repentant sinners with a sordid past into the church has been happening since the beginning of the Church in the book of Acts. Paul, speaking to believers, says that fornicators, adulterers, homosexuals, thieves, drunkards, and a long list of other sinful lifestyles, will not enter the kingdom of God. Additionally, then he says "Moreover so were some of you" (1 Corinthians 6:9-11) - this means that none is better than the other in the next pew. Each church member has one form of dark past or another, reveals Ephesians 2:2, saying those ways "in which you formerly walked according to the course of this world, according to the prince of the power of the air, of the spirit that is now working in the sons of disobedience." The place of worship has constantly been comprised of forgiven sinners from all possible walks of life.

Receive Those Whom Christ Receives

In submission to God, we must receive those who receive Christ. For the Scripture says, *"Whoever believes in him shall not be ashamed... For there is no distinction between Jew and Greek; the same Lord is Lord of all, abounding in riches for all who call on him.... Everyone who calls on the Lord shall be saved" (Romans 10: 11-13)*. We, by the grace of God, should receive the repentant sex offenders and provide for them communion, teachings and opportunities for spiritual growth including service, while keeping the children safe. Meanwhile, the church should also by the grace of God, help those in their midst who have been victims of sexual abuse to heal, grow and be restored. The teachings of the church must mean the same thing to all believers regardless of what their past has been. The church should be a place where all sinners receive forgiveness, acceptance, love, encouragement, fellowship, teaching, and be an integral and vital member of the church. This does not mean that the experience of each church will necessarily be the same. While forgiveness for the repentant soul is unconditional, life in the church may be affected by the consequences of our sins. It is up to believers to forgive as he is forgiven, but where trust is broken, as it has been with sex offenders - confidence needs to be restored, although there are some areas where trust or service opportunities may be lost forever.

More Verses to Show Why We Should Accept Those with Offenses

- *Romans 2:11 - "For God shows no partiality."*
- *1 Corinthians 12:25-26 - "That there may be no division in the body, but that the members may have the same care for one another. If one member suffers, all suffer together; if one member is honored, all rejoice together."*
- *2 Corinthians 2:5-8 - "For such a one, this punishment by the majority is enough, so you should rather turn to forgive and comfort him, or he may be overwhelmed by excessive sorrow. So I beg you to reaffirm your love for him."*
- *Jude 21-23 - "And have mercy on those who doubt; save others by snatching them out of the fire; to others show mercy with fear, hating even the garment stained by the flesh."*
- *Roman 15:1 - "We who are strong have an obligation to bear with the failings of the weak and not to please ourselves."*

Some Biblical Reasons for Setting Limitations

- The Bible points out that sexual sin is different than other kinds of sin; it would seem, according to Paul, that it has a more heinous and demoralizing consequence on our bodies. (1 Corinthians 6:18). Consequently, the way in which we deal with the problem, and the restrictions and safety measures we take with sex offenders will be more unique than might be taken in dealing with other types of sin.
- Boundaries help us escape or flee dangerous or tempting situations. "Run from sexual sin. Every other sin committed by a person is outside the body, but the sexually decadent person sins against his own body." (1 Corinthians 6:18).

Protecting the Congregation

While we should welcome the recipients to Christ, we are still bound to exercise divine wisdom. And although we are bound to forgive we are not necessarily forced to trust blindly. Even if a sex offender may have paid his "debt" to society, certain trust may be lost and may need restoring Hence, they may lose some of the common things other members enjoy like freedoms; such as moving about freely within the church building.

There are other types of sex offenders that the church should also make a special provision for - those who, though possibly not convicted of a crime, have a reputation or repeated instances of inappropriate contact or behavior that constantly make the receiving parties uncomfortable; those who may be "womanizing" or "whorish" and exhibit similar kinds of behavior. These specific measures should be taken with known sex offenders - believers and those whose spiritual state is unsafe as described below:

Risk Assessment

Applications for sexual offenders involved in the church should be reviewed by a trained panel. Each case must be evaluated individually - it should not be a one-size-fits-all approach. Keep in mind that some sex offenders may be more likely to re-offend than others. Some crimes may have been crime displays such as downloading pictures or videos, while other crimes may have involved actual unwelcome physical contact with victims. It is the responsibility of the panel to meet with the offender and others if help is needed in order to understand all the dynamics of the case. "Others" here refer to their probation officer, social worker, and local police; they will assist to determine the severity of the infringement and to get a better idea of the individual.

The panel handling the risk assessment may also benefit from gathering relevant public records from the government group that arrested and acted against the individual. They should also check with the probation providers of the offender to determine if they are meeting all expectations of probation and counseling. If the offender is permitted to partake and enter into an affiliation with the church, this verification should be an ongoing duty of the Risk Assessment Panel (RAP).

Registered sex offenders as well as other former criminals who have come into an affiliation with the church should always be subject to observation and guiding principle for their actions, no matter how long they have attended.

Shepherd the Offender

Along with the willingness of a church to offering the hand of fellowship to a repentant sex offender, it must be a consistent loving support and acceptance. This support has to be informed, managed with understanding and devoid of any sentimentality that could allow unsafe situations. The repentant sex offenders need a committed community of brothers and sisters who are aware of their struggles and willing to challenge actions that could invite temptation. The church should be a place where repentant sex offenders may find encouragement, support, responsibility and respect as they work to rebuild their lives and follow the life of Christ.

Participation/commitment in the following areas have been shown to help sex offenders reduce the risk of re-offending:

- Maximizing potential
- Discovering gifts, talents, and purpose
- The support of family and friends after release
- Connection and participation in a community
- Avoid situations that jeopardizes his or her freedom

- Participation in an ongoing support group/life coaching program (s)
- Agreement to accountability

The above, are areas where the church could play an essential role in the life of a sex offender, through support and responsibility. On every occasion possible the church should seek to come beside the repentant sex offender to assist them in putting the evil elements of wrongdoing behind them.

Nevertheless, while we are working on ministering to sex offenders, we should also not forget the witch-trial-like hysteria fluffed up around hearings regarding allegations in this matter. Many blameless people have had their lives destroyed. All it takes is finger pointing from a student angry at a teacher or step-father, for example, to brand someone for life. Our American systems of jurisprudence has conveyed to the public very little if anything on branding someone for life. People know about the death penalty, life imprisonment, but not release with a brand. Certainly, there are some cases where low standards of evidence have been used, allowing the guilty to go free and the innocent suffer - sometimes for life. In the face of all the controversies associated with the issue, the church should assist in establishing new hope to persons who have committed sexual offenses in the past.

P.O. Box 453

Powder Springs, Georgia 30127

www.entegritypublishing.com

info@entegritypublishing.com

770.727.6517

www.ingramcontent.com/pod-product-compliance
Lightning Source LLC
Chambersburg PA
CBHW050443010526
44118CB00013B/1664